Dare

to

Stimulate

*Anecdotes, Opinions, and Advice to
Awaken Intellectual Curiosities*

RYAN BRUECKNER

DEDICATION

To my wife who understands me.
To my family that makes life worth living.
To my friends that make life memorable.
To those that dare to live and not just breathe.

Table of Contents

INTRODUCTION

⮑⟫⟫⟩⟩⟩⟩⟩⟫⟪⟪⟪⟪⟪⟪⟪⟨⮐

I live the life of a twenty-first century nomad, plain and simple. My personal and professional existences have taken me around the world and afforded me the opportunity to interact and share experiences with some of the most interesting people imaginable. These experiences, along with decades of life lessons and incremental moments, have pushed me into a hobby no one, and I mean no one including myself, saw coming: writing.

Over the span of the past five years, I have spent many moons flying the friendly skies. During my travel, I started to do something and do it religiously: think and write. I am admittedly not a big book reader. I read enough for work to fill a nonexistent library in my house so when it comes to down time I choose to save what's left of these twitchy eyes for other activities. I don't have the attention span to commit to a movie in flight. The flights are either too short to complete a movie, which is one of my biggest pet peeves, or too long and I just need to get up and move. But having a beverage or two while listening to 90s alternative jams and logging intellectual curiosities that pop into my head? Now we are talking.

This habit was originally intended to distract my mind from the workings of a long week. I would order a beverage on a Thursday flight home, fire up a playlist perpetually in need of a desperate update, and write down everything that popped into my mind. That was it. The writing was a simple journaling activity that I unintentionally and unknowingly at the time would grow to truly enjoy. While I have never kept a formal journal, I found the action of writing my thoughts, ideas, opinions, and memories incredibly fulfilling and extremely satisfying.

As the recreational journaling activity progressed through the years, I began to share this declaration of ideas with people close to me. The family or friends with whom I shared my thoughts, laughed with me and at me, but a pattern developed in the way people responded that encouraged me to take a closer look. Many of the ideas in my writing elicited conversations, memories, stories, laughter, surprise, sadness, debate, and even occasional tears. While no one passage or excerpt drew the same interest, the clear majority seemed to stimulate people to think. As I continued writing, I began the daunting task of categorizing my writing based on the type of emotion and reaction they had received, and the excitement for sharing these ideas truly began to form. Upon the completion of this activity, the outcome and intention of this once literary nonsense was clear: if I could stimulate someone's mind to provoke a reaction of any kind, I would satisfy my definition of success, and that's how *Dare to Stimulate* was born.

No rules are associated with this text, but here are some guiding principles:

- Each page should stimulate your mind, if not, move on to a quote, passage, or thought that does.

- While the five sections provide structure for the types of intellectual curiosities you might find relevant in each, nothing should prevent you from loosely engaging with the content. Successful engagement with each topic depends on your state of mind at that moment in time, so you should do what feels natural.

- Challenge the topic, engage with the observation, and allow yourself to reflect, react, and re-engage with yourself and the world around you.

- Lastly, and most importantly, always strive to the best version of yourself every day. No recipe to cracking this damn near impossible task exists, but the following pages may help push you in the right direction.

People come from diverse backgrounds and are driven by unique sets of circumstances and experiences, yet all of our minds can fall victim to repetition and consistent observations determined by our current environment. I dare you to break that mold, if even for a second, and look at yourself and those around you through a slightly different lens. Life is precious, and I hope this book reminds you of that. Enjoy my friends.

CHAPTER 1

ADVICE – RULES OF THE ROAD

You can have your cake and eat it too

Responsibilities of phone call initiators

Weddings are not about the bride and groom

Positive Mental Attitude Is Everything

Never wear white socks with dress shoes

You can have your cake and eat it too

The modern day use of the idiom "you can't have your cake and eat it too" is ridiculous. Are you really trying to tell someone they can't have it both ways? If so, use a different expression. If it's your cake, you absolutely can have it and eat it whenever you damn well please.

Responsibilities of phone call initiators

If a phone call drops, the person who initiated it should call back. This seems to be a subtle yet consistent point of confusion across all people and age groups.

Left lane drivers are a unique bunch

While driving down the freeway listening to "Life in the Fast Lane," remember to cruise in the middle or far right lane unless passing. Those individuals who choose to drive in the left lane are either oblivious or uneducated. If the latter, take this as free advice. If the former, you really need to tighten the screws. The pace of traffic will thank you.

This is my toothbrush. There are many like it but this one is mine

Sharing a toothbrush is unequivocally unacceptable. Share deodorant, share floss, share hair gel, share a razor if you absolutely must but never ever share a toothbrush. Considering the fact that your mouth is a balmy rain forest of growing bacteria, this is one of those rules that everyone should be instinctively aware of and abide by. If you don't have a toothbrush, your finger is an amazing replacement. And, if for some reason you get your hands on my toothbrush thinking I'd be cool with you using it, do both of us a favor and keep it.

Impersonate an accent

Every single person should try and impersonate an accent. Being able to throw out a country "ya'll," an English "cheerio," or an Aussie "g'day, mate" in a moment of needed levity is hilarious to me, especially when the impersonation is just plain terrible.

You are a hypocrite. We are all hypocrites

You are a hypocrite. We all are in some capacity. Staying true to our principles is the struggle between our best and worst sides, and that battle makes us human. Just be sure you have someone to bust your chops and keep you honest once in a while. That's why I chose to get married.

You shouldn't care what people think about you. I couldn't disagree more

People say you shouldn't care what others think about you, I couldn't disagree more. At the very least what people think about you gives perspective on the person you are trying to be and the perception that people have about you. We should all strive toward living a life of our own choosing. Being aware of others' opinions regarding our behavior and impression can help shape how to approach becoming who we eventually want to be.

Positive Mental Attitude Is Everything

Positive Mental Attitude Is Everything. PMAIE. This five-letter acronym has guided me through the journey of life. I have written it on baseball hats, printed it on student government shirts in high school, and written business school essays around its significance. This sacred phrase deserves to be shared with the world. Give it a shot. Who knows, maybe it will work for you. Enjoy and don't take this acronym for granted my friends.

You let me down

Of all the things to say to an individual that can rattle a confident person to the bone, "you let me down" ranks among the top. Not only did you screw up, and I mean really screw up, but the phrasing and potential delivery of the message implies incompetence and lack of trust. No one is perfect, but we should all strive to avoid being associated with those four ego shattering words.

Never be called a liar or cheap

Being called a liar or cheap are the two worst buckets in which to be categorized. Being a liar calls into question an individual's character. Once character has been compromised, regaining trust is virtually impossible. Being called cheap means that you have put others in a difficult situation where they feel they had to make extra financial or emotional effort to either cover or accommodate a choice you made. If you're a liar, good riddance. If you're cheap, there's still hope.

Only say bless you once

Only say bless you once. It's a simple rule but one that avoids annoyance and maintains sincerity.

T-shirt procurement guidelines

T-shirts bought at restaurants and bars are only cool if they're not from the city you reside in. No one ever makes the comment "Wow! I love that t-shirt you bought two blocks from here."

When in doubt, talk about the weather

The best ice breaker of all time between grandparents and grandchildren is the current state of the weather. When in doubt, rain, sunshine, and the changing of the seasons will always strike a common chord.

Sex scenes

No matter your age it will never feel comfortable watching a sex scene in a movie with your parents in the same room. Sorry *Titanic*, you simply are not suitable for our family dinner and movie night.

Weddings are not about the bride and groom

Weddings are not about the bride and groom. Weddings represent a party for all parents involved and their friends. The bride and groom are like a car starter; their involvement is critical, but once the party is initiated, millions of other factors take ownership, priority, and precedent.

Buy a quality briefcase

I appreciate frugality, but do yourself a favor, and buy a quality briefcase. Nothing looks more ridiculous than someone walking into a meeting with either a freebie laptop bag they received at orientation or a briefcase that has holes in it. I'm not saying you need to drop thousands of dollars but find something on the upper end of your budget and remember, stay classy, my friends.

Never wear white socks with dress shoes

White socks should not be worn with dress shoes. Period. Gym? Check. Skate park? Double check. Work? No. Church? Double No.

Let's party

When it comes to the concept of partying and what can be described as "too much fun," ask yourself these questions: What immediate benefit can come from this? Is that benefit going to make me happy in the long run? After this evaluation, if you feel confident with continued indulgence, I say "Party on, Wayne." And you respond with, "<I hope you can fill in the blank>."

Empowering others is critical to leading a team

Empowering others is critical to leading a team and building followership, especially with newbies fresh out of college. If someone doesn't feel they have a say, a voice, or a piece of ownership in what is being delivered, their output will never reach full potential, and a manager will never extract the greatest benefits from their team. Make the investment, be a good coach, and you will forever have a loyal army. If you're the newbie out of college, figure out ways to communicate this message and never forget how you feel once you transition into a managerial role.

Don't ever participate in a Statue of Liberty shot

I had a colleague once suffer from first, second, and third degree burns on his face and chest from participating in a Statue of Liberty shot. Prior to skin grafts, he pleaded with the doctors for any type of home remedy that might help the healing process to reduce the amount of buttock skin that would go on his face (seriously). Their response: protein and water. Over the course of the next two weeks, he consumed pounds and pounds of deli turkey meat and drank gallons of water. When the doctor removed the gauze, the skin on his face was so regenerated they opted not to do the grafts. He now has the same porcelain face he did prior to the incident, except for a small scar on his neck to keep him forever honest. Lesson: don't ever participate in a Statue of Liberty shot, but if you do and burn yourself, protein and hydration can work miracles.

Shower mats should never be soaking wet

Shower mats were invented to give your feet a nice resting place and absorb a small amount of water after you have dried them off. Step one is to turn off the shower. Step two is to wipe the right foot with a towel then place it on the shower mat. Step three is to wipe the left foot with a towel and place it on the mat. I don't know why but roommates and spouses alike choose to skip steps two and three, leaving a soggy, moist mat for anyone who has second dibs on the shower. Gross. Keep it dry, sports fans.

There is a wrong way to open a beer

Bottle openers on key chains are not cool. Bottle openers on the bottom of your Reef sandals are definitely not cool. Bottle openers attached to the inside cargo pocket of your board shorts, really not cool. Opening a bottle of beer with your wedding ring, cool. Opening a bottle with another beer bottle, definitely cool. Opening a bottle of beer with your teeth, really cool. Just make sure you're aware of what side of the "cool" fence you're on at your next tailgate.

Go forth young grasshoppers and tip accordingly

Everyone should know how to calculate 5%, 10%, 15%, and 20% of a given number. This should be a rule that must be learned prior to middle school graduation. For those who are a bit fearful right now, here is an example: Your restaurant bill is $39.23. Round it to $40. The easiest percentage to calculate is 10%. Simply lose the last digit in 40 (which is zero) and voila: you have $4! That trick can be used on any number. Now, let's get real advanced, what's 5% of $40? Well, if 10% is $4 then 5% must be half of that, which equals $2. Now that you have that information, what is 15%? You already have 5% and 10%, so just add them together. Boom! $6. And now for Double Jeopardy, what is 20%? Again, you already have 10%, so just add another

10% to get to 20%. $8! Vanna White congratulates you. Half of you think I'm being a smart ass while the other half of you would never admit it, but you are quietly thanking me. Don't ever admit that you don't know how to do this (ever), but I accept your silent "thank you" and match it with a silent "you're welcome." Now go forth young grasshoppers and tip accordingly!

Our language is not bullet proof

Biweekly or bimonthly confuses the hell out of me. When someone says "biweekly" do they mean twice a week or every other week? The same is true for bimonthly. The definition for biweekly in Merriam-Webster online is "1. Occurring twice a week. 2. Occurring every two weeks." What?! I've always assumed that biweekly meant twice a week, but I have run into several occasions where this was not understood correctly, and rightfully so. Moral of the story is that the English language in not bullet proof. When in doubt, always confirm the meaning behind someone's words.

Wearing sunglasses on a plane is a bit odd

Wearing sunglasses on a plane is a bit odd but mysteriously interesting. Do those people not want to be seen? Are they famous or want to be famous? Do they think sunglasses are similar to an invisible cape that once worn, no one can see them? Or, are they simply suffering from the Sunday withdrawals induced by libations from the night before? The world may never know.

CHAPTER 2

REFLECT – DECODE YOUR PAST

*No one is clever enough to trick what lies in
the bowels of our genetic makeup*

Swallow your self-righteous ego

*I ask you, is it the real world or perceived
world that you live in? Does it matter?*

*Celebrate life so by the time you're dead, you
wouldn't be down to party anyways*

Your body is a miracle

Swallow your self-righteous ego

For those of you with venom in the veins like that of a bark scorpion and who think emotions are for the weak, I respectfully push back and leave you with this: if you haven't had a reason to cry in the last year, you also haven't had a reason to feel true joy. Swallow your self-righteous ego and bring it on in for the real thing. After all, brothers don't shake, brothers hug.

I ask you, is it the real world or perceived world that you live in? Does it matter?

Perception is reality. What an incredibly powerful concept. How we perceive others, and how others perceive us, through our thoughts and impressions often dictates what we think of others on a day-to-day basis. Furthermore, if these perceptions we hold of others become the reality by which we characterize individuals, then does the real world or the perceived world take priority? Like it or not, the impressions people make on us and those we make on others have a great deal to do with our characterization of people. If a person walks into a department store wearing a designer suit instead of sweatpants, that person is perceived to have more money and be more likely to make a purchase. What about the scenario where a person is the last one to exit a building before it blows up? Our perception of others often becomes our reality without even realizing it, that is, our prejudices become how we think. Does a person live in the real world or perceived world? Does it matter?

Aptitude should not be judged by diplomas

Multiple paths to success exist, and thus multiple opinions regarding higher education. I appreciate all opinions on this subject. I like to think of myself in the traditional sense of attending school and the radical sense of doing innovative things that do not require a formal education. Regardless of your appetite for formal education, what seems critically important are the skills and tools a person has learned through trial and error that provide the ability to perform in the professional world. Our professional capabilities should not be judged by the diploma on the wall, but by the quality of craftsmanship demonstrated using those tools and skills regardless of how they were acquired.

Extremists scare the hell out of me

People who live on the extreme ends of the spectrum, including politicians, scare the hell out of me. Do you think extremism is a function of people striving to be outrageously different or a classification for a group of people who genuinely fall into this frightening category? While arguments support both sides, the former seems to be true in my humble and extreme opinion.

Most Formative Actors: Kevin Arnold and Winnie Cooper

If you were of the generation who watched *Saved by the Bell* and *Family Matters* right after school and just before tuning into WGN to watch the Cubbies play, then you must remember *The Wonder Years*. With an opening song, "With a Little Help from My Friends," by Mr. Joe Cocker, I grew to not only love the characters in the show but in some strange way made a connection with them. My life at that time, even though the show takes place in the late 1960s and I was watching it in the 1990s, was like that of the characters in the show. Kevin Arnold was a kid who was just figuring out how the hell to grow up with no playbook on life, and so was I. Winnie Cooper, the all-American girl next door and his forever crush, was tall, pretty, and innocent, so was Jacqueline who lived down the street from me. Kevin and I were the same person! For whatever reason, I still think about that television series from time to time and can't help but to wonder why these similarities resonated with me so powerfully. Was it the fact that my little brain was just fighting to make a connection with something tangible to make sense of my evolving and complicated world? Did I need an escape from losing all my Pugs on the playground earlier that afternoon? Whatever the case, we all have something that reminds us of moments in life where things started to make sense, the world suddenly appeared a little larger than before, and decisions began to have consequences. Take a moment to remember what influenced you at a young age. Was it a show? Was it a song? What made an impression on you? What were you trying to figure out? And, what was it that made it all come together? Remember that moment in time, capture it, and then look at your son, granddaughter, godchild, or niece. What are they trying to figure out? I bet you a slammer and a tube of Pogs that it's not that far from what you were trying to figure out however many years ago…

It was a kinder, gentler time

My mom and dad sometimes refer to their adolescence by saying "it was a kinder, gentler time." What is it about our current time frame that makes our world so different than the time frame our parents grew up in? Assuming each generation's elders have made the same comment since the beginning of time, what time period has led to the most drastic change? What is for certain about this generation is that the world has become an even smaller place. Technology enables us to connect with people and go places unimaginable to previous generations. We have crossed the barrier between reality and a world augmented by algorithms, automation, and predictive analytics. Our social norms are changing the way we interact with and meet people. We have become a smarter group of wandering human beings but at what cost? Social tensions are flagrantly red, government stability is turbulent, and the countries of the world seem to be constantly at odds with one another. But how different is this from the generation who witnessed the production of automobiles and World War I, or those who witnessed a man landing on the moon and the Vietnam War? Were any of these time periods in reality kinder and gentler? Maybe. Maybe not. It's a tough comparison.

Nothing tops Play-Doh

Of all the toys and games, I played with as a child, nothing tops Play-Doh for me. I have no idea why, but I love Play-Doh. The texture, the conformity, and most of all the smell. With all the new gadgets and gizmos available for the young at heart today, my hope is to keep this timeless product alive for the next generation. What is your "Play-Doh" that you hope to champion throughout the years?

No one is clever enough to trick what lies in the bowels of our genetic makeup

Men run on caveman code. The same holds true for women. Some of these instincts are tempered by social norms, but make no mistake, no one reading this book is clever enough to trick his or her inherited genetic makeup as a hand-me-down from our primitive ancestors.

Are you a victim of a bubble?

When I think about what really makes me the kind of mad where I could put my fist through a wall and not feel it, I realize nothing radiates from my mind. This tells me that problems and dissatisfaction are nothing but a culmination of smaller dissatisfactions and life isn't all that bad. Millions of people might reply to a thought like this with a list of things that piss them off, but I guess the world I live in just doesn't have space for that. With the right attitude, more energy can be spent on progressive thoughts, not reactionary ones. I may be a victim of a bubble to some extent, but hey, more power to whatever makes you sleep at night.

People can remain semi-civilized in an environment that is completely isolated

Airline travel cracks me up. People remain semi-civilized in an environment that is completely isolated, putting up with irritating situations, including seat kicking and invasion of personal space. Yet, if someone is delayed for all of two seconds at a stoplight, those same puppet-like people are the ones honking as if a tsunami was approaching. Weird. I know I'm guilty of it. Are you?

George Strait and Ace of Base

The Goo Goo Dolls, Everclear, George Strait, Leon Russell, Ace of Base, Bruce Springsteen, Fragma, and New Kids On The Block are responsible for shaping my keen ear for talented music. Music is more powerful than any combination of words that can be used to describe its effect on the human condition. The connections music makes between the past and present and the emotions it generates are truly food for the soul.

Eye surgery and risk rationalization

LASIK eye surgery seems incredibly exciting and incredibly frightening. The stakes seem low for complication, but the law of large numbers suggests a small percentage of people who have the procedure done will in fact have severe complications. I'm always interested in how people rationalize situations like this. Let's take a scenario where after an eye injury from a car wreck, the doctor asks you this: "Would you rather be guaranteed to have 20/20 vision in only one eye or opt for a progressive surgery that will give you a fifty percent chance of seeing 20/20 in both eyes or a fifty percent chance of not seeing at all?" The variety of replies I have heard to this question are extremely interesting.

Death, suffering, and strength

When my grandmother passed away, I was simultaneously sad and relieved. Watching pain and suffering is the worst part of our human existence. Yet, in some strange, unexplained manner her pain left me feeling slightly stronger than I was before. My grandmother was a class act lady with a heart of gold and a mind as tough as leather. We all know at least one person like this who, through their suffering, left us stronger, more compassionate, and more appreciative. She was and always will be my rock and my savior. Cheers to you and a Pink Squirrel in your honor, Grandma.

Superpowers and your brain

The greatest superpower of all time would be the ability to remember everything you learn, read, watch, and observe. I have spent countless hours relearning and refreshing myself on a myriad of topics and if only I could document all these useful tidbits in my brain. Mastering a superpower may be impossible, but being aware of personal growth opportunities can help a person focus on areas of improvement. The natural questions are: "What superpower do you want, and how can you strive to incorporate it into your life?"

Toes are super weird

Toes are among the strangest appendages I have ever seen on a living creature. The shape, the size, the nail structure, and the position are bizarre. Yet, they are incredibly important for balance, stability, and bearing weight. Our world is filled with oddities that when investigated reveal a deeper, significant meaning. So, I ask you wise sage, what "toes" seem weird to you in your life and what is the purpose? I bet you'll be amazed at what you can find out. Just be sure to cover those bad boys up in a professional setting.

What am I good at? What do I want to do?

On the road to professional success, you should always ask yourself two questions: What am I good at? What do I want to do? Awareness of proficiency provides a person the confidence to perform above expectations and builds trust with those who evaluate you. Awareness of what you want to do allows you to take advantage of new opportunities, learn new skills, and maintain motivation. Ideally you will become good at the things you want to do, thus creating your own arsenal of professional weaponry.

Keystone beer and Silver Oak Cabernet

If your house is stocked with both Keystone beer and Silver Oak Cabernet, you can officially be anointed as a classy fraternity superstar for life. But in all seriousness, don't ever let go of the experiences in your life that got you where you are today. (Mine happen to be surrounded by cheap beer.)

Conceptualizing the element of time

No matter how long someone has lived, it never seems like his or her time should be now. I wonder what that says about our ability to conceptualize the element of time.

Every second we breathe is but a rounding error

If you really want a deep thought, think about your sole purpose on this planet. Who are you now, who do you want to become, and what do you want to accomplish? If every second we breathe is but a rounding error in the grand scheme of our life on this planet, then pick a direction and start marching; you can always pivot a few steps down the path.

Celebrate life so by the time you're dead, you wouldn't be down to party anyways

Funerals are often called a "celebration of life." While that has most certainly been the case at the few I have attended, I can't help but think that the person being buried would have really enjoyed being a part of their celebration. Moral of the story: go out and celebrate life as much as possible so that by the time you're dead, you wouldn't have been down to party anyways.

Mind over matter and porta-putty lines

Not being able to go to the restroom when you need to is a hor-rific and terrible sensation. Road trips with no foreseeable exits, high profile meetings you can't step out of, and outdoor concerts with mile long porta-potty lines are traps that prevent nature from taking its course. But remember, your mind is a powerful thing when exercised correctly. You can alter the physical state of your body through focus and concentration. Next time you find yourself in a position like this, just remember: mind over matter. And, maybe bring some toilet paper while you're at it.

Learning is not binary

Figuring out the best way you learn is one of life's greatest challenges. And, what makes this task even harder is that our best method of learning changes over time. Without question I have become a more visual learner. I used to read instructions on how to put together a piece of furniture, but now I am much more receptive to pictorial representation (I loved that college Ikea stuff). Whether it's visual, audio, written, or kinesthetic, test out different methods of learning and don't be afraid to make a change.

Text messaging has destroyed the English language

When preparing for the infamous GMAT exam (the test you take prior to applying to a post-graduate business program), I found the sentence correction portion to be extremely difficult. I've always fancied myself as a good student of the English language, yet my verbal scores were significantly worse than the verbal section on the SAT test I had taken some ten years prior. What on earth could have caused this dramatic decrease? Answer: text messaging! Text messaging has become a splendid form of communication, but it has destroyed any progress I was making toward improving sentence structure. Just wait until some report surfaces on *60 Minutes* highlighting the significant drop in English proficiency across the country. You can say you heard it here first. As for business school? Sorry Harvard, I gave you my best shot, but I guess I'm just a public-school kid after all.

To burn out or fade away, that is the question

Neil Young stated in his famous song "Hey Hey My My," "It's better to burn out than fade away." For some strange reason this quote has had a significant impact on my life. I think we all straddle the line between running fast, taking chances, and living life to the fullest, while simultaneously feeling the urge to be a bit more cautious, to stop and smell the roses, and to live life a little more safely. Deep down, I want a life of safety (who doesn't?!), but I absolutely want to soak up everything life has to offer in a "guns a-blazin" approach. This puts me somewhere on the path to either complete self-destruction by fifty years old, or an 85-year-old man filled with life stories for all who will listen. If I had to make a choice one way or the other, let's burn out baby and hope for the best. Regardless of your appetite for risk tolerance, just be damn sure to live life with no regrets.

People who marry you and bury you

Who are the friends who will marry you and bury you? This question came up repeatedly during my fraternity pledgeship, and I never really thought much about it until now. Of all the people who will come in and out of your life, a select few will be in it for the long haul. Give one of them a call right now just to say hello. Why the hell not?

If you really don't know the difference, then what difference does it make?

For all you steak eaters out there, what steak do you typically order? Filet? New York Strip? Sirloin? Porterhouse? Prime Rib? But do you legitimately understand the difference between the steaks, other than their prices? It is a shocking truth that most people have no idea. Different steaks represent different cuts of meat. And those different cuts have different tastes and different recommended ways to cook each. Truth be told, I really don't know the differences between all the different cuts, just that I like filets. Bottom line: order what you want, but if you really don't know the difference, then what difference does it make?

Your body is a miracle

Your body is a miracle! My senior year of college I took a sexual education class, which I thought would be entertaining on several levels, with a bunch of my friends. Little did I know that we would ride a slender yet powerful flagellum on a crash course throughout the entire human body. Our professor ended each class with the entire section repeating after him, in unison, "My body is a miracle!" I thought it was super creepy yet hilarious at the time, but the more you learn about the body, conception, and how scientifically unique you are, the more you realize that, yes, I guess I really am a miracle! We won't be covering sex education in this book, but suffice to say the body truly is a miracle. You should feel privileged.

CHAPTER 3

RESPECT –
HONOR YOURSELF
AND OTHERS

Adderall will be the worst drug of our generation

Goosebumps are among the great mysteries of the human body

Your body is a battery that needs to be recharged

Stand in the middle of your spotlight

Wine labels define excellence

Adderall will be the worst drug of our generation

When most of us think of vices or addictive substances, we think of hard drugs like meth, heroin, cocaine, and in some situations alcohol. They are undoubtedly toxic and destructive, not only to the abuser but to all the people around the addicted person. But the drugs mentioned are not the only substances abused today. There is a new culprit spreading like fire and that drug is Adderall. Adderall is a substance that is easily accessible and often condoned by parents and physicians in the name of "focus". This stimulant, often prescribed for Attention Deficit/Hyperactivity Disorder (ADHD) and narcolepsy, is overprescribed, used more recreationally than any medication I have observed, and serves as a crutch when people need to focus fully. Adderall allows people to maintain day-to-day functionality at a stimulated level, which is a frightening differentiator in comparison to vices that prevent such efficiency. Like other prescribed drugs, obtaining a prescription is just a doctor visit away, and the intended versus actual use are very different for many users. Adderall is just one example of a modern and accessible vice that is affecting many children, young adults, and parents. While we do not know the long-term effects of this drug (or many others for that matter), tread cautiously with substances you put in your body. Consider the fact that alternative vices (e.g., relationship issues or work performance) may be holding you back, and no drug will fix these problems. Drugs serve as a numbing agent until an addiction is formed.

Stand in the middle of your spotlight

I am impressed by people with influence. They are not any better than you or me, but they figured out where their spotlight was shining and how to stand directly in the middle of it. That to me is impressive.

Write someone a letter

Writing letters by hand is nearly a forgotten past time. If you're even a remote member of today's society and have access to the internet or a mobile phone, an email or text message to a friend or family member wishing them happy birthday is quick and reliable and shows the other person you care. But what about the effort that goes into mailing a card or God forbid a letter? Between writing a meaningful message, retraining your hand to focus on penmanship, and buying postage, the many logistical steps involved in the process will contribute to the imminent extinction of this activity. But before you agree to archive this lost art into your primitive category on your bookshelf, think about the last time you received a card. How did it make you feel? Who sent it? For what occasion? I challenge you to send one letter or card to someone special in your life for a momentous occasion. The additional effort required may reinvigorate the passion and care only found in the written word.

You do you. I'll do me

One of the most interesting and thoughtful coworkers I have ever met summarized her complex and intriguing philosophies, lifestyle choices, and personal and professional awareness by simply stating, "You do you. I'll do me." What a brilliant remark.

Opposing positions are welcomed if presented tastefully

Pink and red Starburst are incredible, and orange is all right. Yellow has no business even being mentioned much less distributed with such classy candy siblings. While I'm clearly passionate about my Starburst options, I'm even more intrigued by the person who can make a compelling case to convince me otherwise. These are the types of people who irritate the hell out of me, but I end up growing to respect them. I'm not saying everyone needs to get in my face about Starburst, but opposing positions if presented tastefully are always welcomed.

Breaking points and mental conditioning

A breaking point is nothing more than a measurement on a sliding scale of mental sanity at any given point in time. Imagine two people running a marathon. Imagine they are physically identical. Yet, one person falls to the ground at mile eighteen, and the other finishes the race. Why is this? Mental conditioning. The power of the mind separates losers from winners and the weak from the strong. Always be aware of your mental condition and how to leverage its full potential so that your breaking point never occurs.

Political capital

Political capital is the most powerful asset to have in the workplace. Raise it through hard work and earned respect, and never ever take it for granted. The workplace can take on many forms, and developing and growing your political capital will behoove you when you least expect it.

Pachamama

Plastic goods are used daily in our lives. From grocery bags to toys, this material can be molded into many different objects. But when you look at the environmental damage plastic causes, you see that this synthetic compound is like plaque to human arteries. You can try and clean it up, but it never quite goes away. Now I'm not here to preach environmentalism, but take a moment to hit the recycle bin on your way out. It's important to become aware of the effects we have on our surroundings and how we can prolong this beautiful thing called mother earth as we become a more sophisticated and advanced society.

The world needs more hugging and less hurting

Make a pact with yourself to continue being a student of and teacher to the community. The world needs more hugging and less hurting, and making an impact on your community is an easy and simple starting point. If giving back must start some-where, what better place than right here, right now.

Reputations exist for a reason

Reputations exist for a reason. Be aware of them, challenge them, and in certain situations try to disprove them. You will be a far more unbiased, informed, and respected person for doing so.

Look left. Look right

Focus on helping people to your left and right. While making contributions and assisting foundations or organizations that support both domestic and foreign causes are critically important, we would all be shocked by how much the people to whom we are closest may need help. This realization occurred to me after a conversation with a close friend who appeared happier than my dad eating on Thanksgiving but deep down was destroyed and yearning for some advice from a trusted friend. This individual, ironically, is one of the greatest philanthropists I know, unselfishly giving his time and money to charities of all kinds around the world. My takeaway from this experience is to focus on helping those around you. The dialogue is meaningful, the situation is real, and the bond created, which often goes untapped in friendships and relationships, is undoubtedly special. Maybe the people we help will have the greatest chance of making a global difference; they just needed a bit of clarity from the person standing next to them.

Wine labels define excellence

Ordering wine at dinner is like buying clothes at a department store: the raw materials are nearly identical but the label separates mediocrity from excellence. All that being said, the best type is the one you like.

Goosebumps are among the great mysteries of the human body

Goosebumps are among the great mysteries of the human body. These little bumpy creatures can take over entire or partial parts of the body and are activated through physical and nonphysical contact. The physical contact is a little easier to grasp. Tickle the back of someone's arm or blow on the back of a person's neck and voila, goosebumps. But the nonphysical aspect is a pure mystery. What causes me to connect a song, a feeling, a thought to some part of my brain that stimulates goosebumps? In a world where people are seemingly numb, pay attention to what activates your body. Maybe you're more alive than you realize.

Bring it on in for the real thing

Giving someone you care about a hug is the most sincere expression of caring and compassion that does not cross the line of inappropriate behavior.

Do not pop pills

Do everything you can to avoid popping prescription or over-the-counter pills. Dependencies on medications can make the body weak and the mind dull. If this is not an option, then educate yourself on what you're taking and constantly self-evaluate your dosage and frequency. Medication is a beautiful thing for short-term illnesses or chronic conditions, but far too many people have made this a part of their daily intake without testing alternative methods. You have one body, take care of it.

Every decision has an impact on your life

Every decision has an impact on your life. Every single one. The sooner you realize this, the more you will appreciate how fortunate you are to have good intuition, instinct, and gut reaction.

Rich and filthy rich

"How much money did you make on the transaction?" I asked. "Well, let's put it this way, I walked away with a few commas," he replied. If that's not a reply from a straight-up business boss, then I don't know what is. And to make matters even more ridiculous, he was one of the most polite and cordial people I have ever met. There are filthy rich assholes out there, and then there are filthy rich badasses. That gentleman is a badass.

Friends and homecoming kings

Regardless of your relationship or dependent status, finding time to connect with your friends is critical. Maybe you have one solid friend, or maybe you've been able to maintain your homecoming king status and have hundreds. Whatever the number is, make it a point to see those individuals once a year.

Respect your parents

Respect your parents. They're the only ones you have. The simple fact that they brought you into this world is a ridiculous miracle, and if you happen to like them, life is a hell of a lot easier too.

Your body is a battery that needs to be recharged

Sleep is vitally important to your well-being. If you don't get enough sleep, all aspects of your life will be affected. Imagine walking into work with two hours of sleep while everyone else has averaged seven to eight hours. Now consider that same scenario Monday, Tuesday, and Thursday over an entire year. Your body is a battery that needs some recharge time and depriving that battery of idle rest can have lasting consequences. Be sure to carve out time for quality rest regardless of age. My grandfather was a pro at this.

Teams and individuals thrive when respect is present and agreed upon

Surround yourself with people who have different beliefs, ideas, interests, approaches, and backgrounds. I have found that diverse groups who have true respect for one another can generate solutions to some incredibly complex and damn near impossible problems. An intelligent and motivated group of people, who may only agree on treating each other with respect, can do some remarkable things.

CHAPTER 4

PRIDE – LOVE YOURSELF AND WHERE YOU CAME FROM

The daily privilege of aging

In a world filled with unpredictability have a cup of coffee

Be selfish. If you won't someone else will

*Firm handshakes, eye contact, and
enthusiastic storytelling will prevail*

Never underestimate the importance of getting your hair cut

Find your place of peace

I enjoy places that are frozen in time, where the pace is a little slower, people give an honest wave as they drive by, and the buildings, roads, and décor have what I can only describe as character. If I close my eyes, these places make me think about my generation, my parents' and grandparents' generations, and how we all would have coexisted if given the opportunity. Permanently transitioning to a place like this is not on my priority list, but knowing it exists brings me a comforting sensation of peace. I encourage you to find your place of peace.

Extracurricular activities are extremely influential

Extracurricular activities are extremely influential, especially for young people. Regardless of the activity, whether sports, theater, art, or community service, extracurricular activities are an incredible crash course in lessons of success and failure and how to manage emotions, people, and responsibilities. Some of my greatest memories and best friendships were formed in the Arizona heat on the soccer and baseball fields. I attribute my sense of discipline and competitive spirit to these recreational activities and can confidently say I'm a better person for having participated. If I could say "thank you" to each coach, teammate, or mentor I participated with I would, but I'll have to settle for promoting extracurricular involvement for generations to come as a form of payback.

Hand surgeons and professional athletes are among the most talented people in the world

A brilliant vice chairman at an investment bank in New York City once told me that hand surgeons and professional athletes are among the most talented people in the world. The skills required to perform a successful hand surgery without jeopardizing the approximately twenty-seven bones that tightly make up hand functionality is nothing short of a miracle. The same story holds true for the probability of playing professional sports. As I sat listening to this finance tycoon, who I thought was the true definition of talent, I found that his comments really pissed me off. "I could have been a professional athlete" or "If I dedicated myself to medicine, I could've become a hand surgeon." This guy didn't even consider himself or his profession in his remarks! For whatever reason I wrote down hand surgeons and athletes in my MBA branded padfolio and would revisit that comment throughout the year as I pursued the daunting task of switching careers as an MBA student. Why hand surgeons and professional athletes? Many moons later, when I was not pursuing a career in investment banking, I realized the reason behind my disappointment and irritation. I didn't like his definition of talent. Because I held this individual in such a high regard, I attempted to fit his mold when I clearly did not agree with it. Be genuine with your feelings and your own definitions of talent in this world. The talent you are seeking to emulate may simply be your own reflection in the mirror.

Never underestimate the importance of getting your hair cut

I look forward to getting my hair cut. It gives me confidence, a positive self-image, underpins my belief in professionalism, and simply makes me feel good. Never underestimate its importance. And for God's sake enjoy a beer or glass of wine if the opportunity presents itself. After all, what better way to celebrate than a toast to yourself as you stare in an awkward mirror with a random human touching your hair for an extended period of time.

Make your bed every morning

You should make your bed every morning. It is a quick and easy win and amazingly instills a sense of organization, discipline, and pride.

You don't cry? Figure out why and make a change

If you don't tear up at some point during the Super Bowl, The Masters, the movie Armageddon, or the thought of the American flag, you should figure out why and potentially make a change. Tears shed in the name of sentimental value wake up the soul, stimulate the mind, and reconnect the body with an incredible stockpile of dormant emotions. Find your sentimental trigger and don't be afraid to let the tears flow like the salmon of Capistrano.

Arizona, Texas, and the life of a twenty-first-century nomad

I have spent most of my life in Arizona and Texas. I love them both. Arizona's painted desert filled with saguaro cacti and surrounding mountains and valleys is the place I imagine when I close my eyes. The endless plains and beautiful hill country of Texas overwhelm me with comfort and warmth. I have been fortunate to travel to many parts of the world, but these two incredible states are home. With travel becoming more accessible, and affordable in certain cases, many of us live a life of a twenty-first-century nomad, hopping from place to place, and often spending several weeks a year away from our overpriced bed mattresses. But with all this hustle and bustle I ask you, where is home to you and what makes it special?

Firm handshakes, eye contact, and enthusiastic storytelling will prevail

I am a people pleaser, plain and simple. My view is that the benefits of having people like me far exceed the laundry list of negative remarks people have towards people pleasers. I guess we'll find out in the end. Until then, firm handshakes, eye contact, and enthusiastic storytelling will continue to prevail.

Few things remain one hundred percent pure

There are very few things that remain one hundred percent pure. Family is pure. Value your family and don't ever let them slip in the long list of priorities we have.

Be selfish. If you don't someone else will

It's okay to be selfish once in a while. How can you possibly learn to look out for and take care of others if you haven't taken care of yourself? It's not popular to be self-serving, but in moderation it is absolutely necessary.

People in the military are badasses

People in the military are badasses. The thought of people spending part or all of their professional career in an organization designed to defend the homeland is foreign to me and what I have done thus far. Although serving in the military has most certainly passed me by due to age and a gnarly meniscus tear, I whole heartedly support our protectors and would like to think that my service will come soon enough in a different form (presidential campaign 2036?). My hope is that each individual has a desire and passion to give back to this incredible country. We need intelligent, dedicated, and goal-oriented people to continue America's path to greatness, and I hope that person is you.

In a world filled with unpredictability have a cup of coffee

A cup of coffee represents the beginning to a new day. In a world filled with unpredictability, I always find comfort in things simplistic and consistent.

Traveling as much as you can might just make you realize how good you have it

Traveling internationally does two things for me. It makes me realize how drastically different my world is from that of others and confirms my opinion that I love living in America. These are not simple times. Exploring as much as you can might just provide a much needed change in perspective.

Always remember to be cool

As you get older, sacrifice cool for practical, but always remember to stay a little cool.

The daily privilege of aging

The aging process is a cruel and unavoidable part of life. Some begin this process much earlier while others seem to have a front of the line pass to the fountain of youth as described in *Bridge to Terabithia*. Either way the years will go by, the skin will change, and the mind will dull. But I choose to view this cruelty as more of a badge of honor. Longevity in this world is not guaranteed, and each day should be met with gratitude and thankfulness for taking yet another breath of air, regardless of the consequences that come with this daily privilege.

Be the best version of your true self

Pretending to be someone different than who you are is not sustainable. Sure, we all enjoy that moment where people laugh and gravitate toward the best image of our pretend self, but the energy exerted is not natural and can become very tiresome. Be the best version of your true self. That is all anyone can ask.

You're cut from a different cloth

One of my favorite expressions of all time is "that person is cut from a different cloth". How in the world did a piece of cloth get caught up in the mix? But in all seriousness, I could not think of a better compliment. Be a little weird, be a little different, and challenge the status quo. Life is insanely short. If you're cut from a different cloth, I'd like to check it out some time.

Eye contact is critical

Eye contact is critical. I don't care how young you are or how little experience you have, nothing rattles the lack of confidence radar more than wandering eyes. Be confident, comfortable, and pretend you have something meaningful to say until you actually do.

CHAPTER 5

ACT – DO OR DO NOT, THERE IS NO TRY

Grip and rip is universally applicable

Taking action depends on the lens you use and the maturity of those optics

One word and its very self-explanatory: sweat

I just saved you $150,000 in graduate school fees

Become a jack of many trades and a master of few

Taking action depends on the lens you use and the maturity of those optics

Telling yourself to take a chance is easy. Telling someone else to take a chance is even easier. The action ultimately is the only thing that matters. That action can be the easiest or hardest thing to do in the world. It simply depends on the lens you use and the maturity of those optics.

One word and its very self-explanatory: sweat

I am starting to realize how important fitness is and its correlation with health, happiness, and success. I have always tried to make fitness a part of my daily life (some years have been better than others), but my intentions have changed in recent years. I spent more than thirty years slamming weight gainer shakes in hopes of relinquishing my beanstalk title, and now I can only hope to preserve it. Unless you believe you're coming back to this world in a different form, we all have one shot at this life, and I don't know about you but waking up every morning is pretty sweet. How does one stay physically fit to promote a long and healthy life? How does one make such a drastic change? One word and it is very self-explanatory: sweat.

There are only good and great days

You should strive to have good and great days; anything less is a waste of time.

Grip and rip is universally applicable

The term "grip and rip" is universally applicable. From baseball to the farm to the business world, this term can be used in a million different ways so long as the intended use has a desirable outcome. Now go "grip and rip."

The balancing act of work and life

Work-life balance is an odd concept to me. I view work deliverables and related tasks to be areas of professional growth. Professional growth fuels motivation, creativity, and the desire to improve. Having the motivation and desire to push the envelope in the working world shapes who I am in my personal world. My personal life allows me to reap the benefits from hard work and success and forms things like confidence, satisfaction, and the burning desire to achieve life goals and dreams. Thus, the process is iterative and not mutually exclusive. Work and personal life are integrated components and balancing them is simply an indicator of satisfaction with the current state of myself.

Feelings are impressionable. Act accordingly

One of the greatest quotes was said by Maya Angelou, "People will forget what you said, people will forget what you did, but people will never forget how you made them feel." Feelings are impressionable. Act accordingly.

We are all creatures of habit

We are ALL creatures of habit. No matter how much we think we can change, transformation is not simple. If you want to make a change, strap on the boxing gloves and fight for it. I guarantee you'll take it to the twelfth round.

I just saved you $150,000 in graduate school fees

Standardized tests, such as the ACT, SAT, LSAT, GMAT, and MCAT, are ridiculous. They really are. Having said that, I don't have a solution that is ultimately better. Accept them, crush them, and if you don't, figure it out. Undergraduate and graduate programs are but one platform to absorb a wealth of knowledge. Figure out what you're passionate about, find a path to become the best at whatever you choose, and crush every opportunity you have. Identify mentors to learn the good, the bad, and the ugly and find ways to work the system in your favor. The most successful people I have met create opportunities for themselves and are extremely self-aware. If you can be good at one of those and excellent at the other, I just saved you $150,000 in graduate school fees. No need to say thank you, just don't forget the small people like me when you're flying high.

Passion can be a real conundrum

Passion in times of clarity is so tangible it almost becomes an ornate object. But passion in times of confusion serves more as an indescribable force we rely on to break on through to the other side.

Focusing on efficiency can literally change your life

Focusing on efficiency can literally change your life. Find one task or build upon one additional skill to make your job or daily activities more streamlined. Seems simple, but the results will make life even simpler.

Push yourself until you feel physically uncomfortable

Push yourself until you feel physically uncomfortable once in a while. The natural rush experienced from fear and accomplishment leave you significantly more alive and aware.

Intangible currency

In the competitive world in which we live, many of us focus our efforts on improving skills that our friends and peers possess. While this can be self-satisfying and undoubtedly important, what skill can you develop that others don't have? The more we can distinguish ourselves with unique traits the more we will stand out. To put it simply, make yourself valuable in a currency that doesn't exist.

Make this moment successful

The progression of life is determined by a handful of moments that either have a successful or unsuccessful outcome. If you're on board with that, then take it upon yourself to make this moment one of the most successful in your life.

Walk in like you own the place

Some people walk into a room and instantaneously have a presence. What is it about them that gives them a sunburst of radiating energy while everyone else blends in with the wall paper? The difference is that these people walk in a room and act like they own the place. They walk and talk in a manner that makes them instantly appealing to the onlooker. If that's your goal, find your swagger and present yourself as important. Give the audience a confidence they otherwise wouldn't expect, and soon you will see how differently people treat you.

You define leadership

Leadership does not define an individual; the individual defines leadership.

Stop complaining and get a hobby

Job satisfaction is a constant struggle for millions of people around the world. The reality of everyday life (e.g., kids, mortgage, and work) prevents most people from pursuing their dreams. I'd like to say, "to hell with it, follow your passions!" but that is simply not the reality in which most of us live. I believe the bigger issue for most people is finding anything they are passionate about.

How many people complain about their job and financial obligations yet are painfully limited in activities they pursue outside of work? I acknowledge that the daily grind prevents many of us from being Peter Pan in Neverland, but surely everyone can do something to provide themselves a sense of happiness, if even for an isolated moment each week. Here's a brilliant idea, stop complaining and get a hobby.

Become a jack of many trades and a master of few

Many people believe that if you are jack of many trades you are a master of none. But I believe you can become a jack of many trades and a master of few. This way no one can ever criticize you for being broad without depth or narrow without reach.

Educate yourself on religion

Educate yourself on religion. More people have died in the name of religion than any other cause. To claim a religious or nonreligious affiliation is an individual choice, but it is critically important to be informed. Those people that feel the need to push their religious agenda should be able to defend their position with tolerance for differing opinions.

Ask for feedback from colleagues early and often

Ask for feedback from colleagues early and often. Misalignment between expectations often leads to poor performance and can easily be avoided through early discussion during any process. The key to avoiding continued performance issues is to harness the early feedback and course-correct accordingly.

Build on your strengths, don't waste your time trying to improve upon your weaknesses

Focus on improving your strengths, not your weaknesses. Your strengths will take you much further in the short and long run.

Do it until it hurts and do it some more

"Do it until it hurts and do it some more." A famous quote from a brilliant man that I choose to live my life by every day. We are all capable of reaching our maximum potential, but the onset of any type of physical or emotional pain prevents some people from doing so. Do not ever let pain get in the way of reaching your climax.

Never be replaceable

"Let's say you are about to start a company and have to fill a critical job position before you make your next billion dollars. What would be your job description?" I was asked this in an interview and came up with the following on the spot, completely plagiarizing the famous Volkswagen commercial, "On the road of life there are passengers, and there are drivers. Drivers wanted." I remember how ridiculous I felt the moment the phrase left my mouth, but to my surprise, the interviewer loved it. Looking back, it's actually not far from the messaging I would include in such a description. I have spent my professional career on two very opposite sides of the professional spectrum: the start-up world and the professional services world. The one common denominator is that the drivers make things happen while the passengers contribute but are replaceable. No matter what you do in life, never be replaceable.

ABOUT THE AUTHOR

Ryan Brueckner was born and raised in Scottsdale, Arizona. He attended the University of Texas and received both his Bachelor of Business Administration and Master of Business Administration from the McCombs School of Business. Ryan has primarily focused on the technology, media, and telecommunications industries and has a dynamic background as both an entrepreneur and a management consultant. He currently resides in Austin, Texas with his family.